Spring's Assurance

Majestic Reflection
Devotional Study Series - Book Two

A quarterly devotional by:

J. K. Sanchez

All scripture quotations are taken from The ESV Bible (The Holy Bible, English Standard Version).

Spring's Assurance: Book 2 of Majestic Reflection Devotional Study Series.
ISBN -13: 978-0692364765
ISBN – 10: 0692364765
Copyright © 2015 by J. K. Sanchez.
Published by: Button Lane Books Spanaway, WA 98387
Contact: Judy@jksanchez.com - www.jksanchez.com

Cover Photography by:
Majestic Reflection-J.K.Sanchez Photography
Cover Design by:
Turtleshell Press www.turtleshellpress.com

Dedication

To those who have begun and continue to walk on this narrow path of stepping into a life journey of pursuing the presence of our Lord Jesus Christ above all other life distractions. Enjoy the journey to living in an assurance of HIS extravagant, unconditional, favor-filled, poured out love for YOU!

Contents

Acknowledgments

First and foremost, I am thankful for the support and consistent overflow of love from my husband, Dennis, my children, their spouses and my grandchildren. When the assurance of the unconditional love of Jesus was ignited within me, His gifts – that are all wrapped up in each of you - my family – were expressions of His love for me. I am forever thankful for each of you.

My continued love and appreciation to my sister, my friend, my almost TWIN in every way and <u>my editor</u>. Thank you Donna for always being there and knowing my thoughts before I speak them.

I am thankful to my friends Christine & Joy. You have been my encouragers and cheerleaders through this whole process of "when pigs fly"; YES this one can. You both make me smile and know that God is on my side "all the time"!

With gratitude and awe I thank-you pastors' Jim & Lorelei for your inspiration that has been the catalyst which allowed this caterpillar to become a butterfly. The Holy Spirit ignited the very inspiration for this series, as I learned to "Hear it" and "Do it" sitting under your words.

And finally – but above all – my thanks to Jesus Christ who directed, inspired, and taught me (step by step) that His love is an assurance I can stand-on. His presence and promise of favor and abundance are always there for me.

My life is not my own but a gift freely given back to the one who gave His life for me.

Introduction

My passionate journey for the presence of the Lord began within me decades ago and has drawn me to a narrow path filled with promise and freedom that I have never experienced before. During this journey I have found a deep <u>knowing</u> of my true identity as a daughter of the King and His amazing love for ME. As my path has narrowed to a place of the <u>one thing</u> – His face and presence - I have learned a new depth of love, rest, new life, joy and the importance of simplification that has brought me the true freedom of Christ.

His gift on the cross is just that – a gift. All of the "I can do's" are learning to lie down as my life is becoming focused on Him and what has already been "done" for me.

This book series has been ignited directly from that love and I desire to share, direct and encourage you to a place to meet Him, love Him, hear Him, see Him and be a lover of His presence as I am.

Most devotionals are 365 days of amazing deep thoughts that honestly, most of us don't make through. We miss a few days and give it up.

This devotional study series is:

Based on a **quarter** and a 6-day week; (leaving day 7 for you to experience the filling of His presence as you gather with others).

It is **perpetual** so it can be used year after year as you walk out this journey.

It is **interactive** – it gives you a comparatively thought filled piece of writing and then builds with scripture and questions that will stir you to look deep within yourself - making this a personal growth experience.

My desire is to direct you to His feet and see His transformation materialize in your life.

ENJOY THIS AMAZING JOURNEY OF LIVING IN THE ASSURANCE OF HIS LOVE FOR YOU!

Winter's Thaw – "Some People Are Worth Melting For"

For generations fairy tales have captured our hearts; the hero's, princess's, prince's and villains but today a recent award-winning story is part of my contemplation. We can often find spiritual meaning in the natural as well as in our beloved fairy tales.

The thaw of winter begins deep within the frozen ground where seeds ready for germination rest and wait. The stirring within the seed begins and its purpose pulses – ready for eruption.

Just as the frozen winter ground accepts the suns caressing rays of warmth in order to begin that thaw; often we find ourselves frozen inside, waiting and needing some way to begin the thawing of our hearts.

We find ourselves frozen by fear. Who we are is trapped inside with no escape from the storms that rage continually within. Fear has become our only companion; causing anger, bitterness and condemnation to reign and our hearts become frozen and hard. We tell ourselves to "conceal, don't feel, don't show, don't let them in, don't let them see". We fear that who we are just isn't good enough.

The reality is that just as Olaf said "some people are worth melting for" and Anna sacrificed herself with an act of true love to unfreeze her sisters heart; we have a true sacrifice of love given for us at the cross of Christ.

If you "let it go" and accept one ray of His love you can say good-bye to your past.

Jesus provided one act of sacrificial love that will thaw your frozen heart and the "first time in forever" you will walk through an open door filled with love and acceptance for who you are. The past will not haunt you ever again, as you draw into the warmth of Christ. In the presence of His loving warmth the fear, condemnation, anger and bitterness will melt.

Spring will break forth over you. Who you are and all that you are capable of becoming will begin to erupt just as the warming seeds begin to germinate into the beauty that is encapsulated within them.

Step into His warmth, "let it go" and allow His love to melt the frozen parts of your heart.

Day 1

Journaling – writing down your thoughts, frustrations, God conversations, questions, desires, dreams and beyond is an important discipline to all areas of growth in our lives. This devotional will encourage that thought process. So write, write and write. Get a separate journal notebook and be prolific in your thoughts. Amazing things jump from the Holy Spirit out on to the page as we express ourselves.

Spend some time contemplating what *Winter's Thaw – "Some People Are Worth Melting For."* means to you.

1. What does this mean to you?

2. How does it apply to your life?

Day 2

Jesus' unconditional poured-out love for us was shown as he chose to give His life away to free us from our sins – all of them – past, present and future.

John 3:16 - "For God so loved the world, that he gave his only Son, that whoever believes in him should not perish but have eternal life."

2 Corinthians 5:17 - Therefore, if anyone is in Christ, he is a new creation. The old has passed away; behold, the new has come.

1. Have you said "good bye" to your past and laid it at the feet of Jesus? Take time with Jesus today to be free of the "baggage" from your past.

Whether you have just decided that it was time to lay your past down and accept His free gift* or you have known Christ for many years; contemplate that gift and the victory it has brought to your life.

2. What does His gift of salvation mean in your life today?

*(Accepting Jesus is simply acknowledging your sin and need for forgiveness. Asking Him to forgive you and believing He died for you, that he forgives you, loves you and has the very best in store for you. It's that simple. Welcome to the Kingdom of God!)

Day 3

A frozen heart often goes unknown because the creeping tentacles of fear sneak in. Fear immobilizes us and our ability to move into all of what God has planned for our lives becomes frozen. Those fears can be honest fears such as health concerns, finances and family. But also fears of our past history, of what others think of us, or just not being good enough to do "whatever" your desires are or Gods stirring and direction.

I John 4:18 - There is no fear in love, but perfect love casts out fear…

1. Consider this scripture in the light of fears that may have snuck into your life.
   What fears have immobilized you?

2. Immobilization only takes a wiggle to break. Chose one fear to wiggle out of today and take a step forward.

3. Memorize this scripture to fight back those fears.

Day 4

The whispers of our past haunt us all and often allow an open door for fear to reign. Jesus shattered and melted away all your past. Allow His love to reign victoriously in your life.

Romans 8:1 - There is therefore now no condemnation for those who are in Christ Jesus.

1. Walking without condemnation requires a knowing of who you are in Christ. Journal your thoughts today of your understanding of who you are as a child of the King?

Day 5

Freedom from fear and condemnation will allow a thawing of your heart in areas that have been frozen. With that thawing will come a pulsing from deep within that will begin to drive forward the purposes and plans that God has placed within you. Decide today to "Let it go". Rejoice in His freedom.

Psalm 23:6 - Surely goodness and mercy shall follow me all the days of my life, and I shall dwell in the house of the Lord forever.

Psalm 86:5 - For you, O Lord, are good and forgiving, abounding in steadfast love to all who call upon you.

Take some time today and rejoice in His goodness, mercy and forgiveness.
1. If fear was not an issue, what has God been stirring within you to do?

2. How could you step forward to see that come to fruition?

Day 6

Re-read *Winter's Thaw* – *"Some People Are Worth Melting For."*

1. What have you learned this week about walking in freedom from fear?

2. What are the keys for you to stay free from condemnation and fear?

Through Christ you reign in Freedom!

The Fog Veil Was Torn

In nature we find veils of fog in many places. Today, two bring me to contemplate a comparison of nature versus spiritual.

A misty veil of fog slowly materializes on the earth causing a nearly silent enclosure. This can be life threatening if you happen to be the captain of a ship at sea.

A veil of fog also slowly materializes over our eyes as we age, causing cataracts that though not life threatening can destroy clarity of vision and disrupt life.

Just as that veil of fog settles over the land and a cloudy cataract enshrouds our eye, so can a clouding slip over our heart.

In the natural we have designed fog horns to loudly cut through the fog and signal those at sea the proximity of danger; thus giving them hope and safety.

A cataract is now removed during a swift surgery that cracks the offensive cloudy lens and places a new clear one, thus allowing a previously veiled eye to see with new clarity the world that was veiled.

Often we are living a life unaware of a fog that has drifted over our heart and eyes. We live a life filled with daily survival.

When we see Jesus for the 1st time, we hear the foghorns signal; hope and forgiveness rush in and safety is found. However, there is so much more. Distractions seem to catch us all unaware, just as the fog on the road or the cataract in our eye.

Jesus sacrifice tore the veil – the fog – between heaven and earth, pouring forth the very breath of God that is available to you. This breath is much more then forgiveness, it's a new life filled with ALL His promises and favor. <u>Jesus bought you a brand new life</u>.

He replaced the foggy lenses of your eyes with crystal clear ones that can see with newfound clarity. This brightness of vision is filled with the destiny that was given to you at your birth.

Due to distractions of life you find that fog has quietly taken over your once joy filled walk with Jesus; your vision has faded, and you are firmly embedded in this drifting fog bank. Much of your clarity and promise of destiny has been swallowed up.

Just as the removal of a cataract is a swift procedure so is the restoration of all that was given to you. His favor is always available and the removal of that fog can dissipate in an instant by looking up to the Son.

Remember the veil was torn for you!

Allow new birth and revelation of His love to erupt over your heart and eyes. It will bring renewal to what has been covered and an awakened stirring of new sight and direction. His plans and purposes for you will begin to be seen as clarity resurfaces.

Day 1

Spend some time contemplating what *The Fog Veil Was Torn* means to you.

1. What does this mean to you?

2. How does it apply to your life?

Day 2

Jeremiah 29:11 – For I know the plans I have for you, declares the Lord, plans for welfare and not for evil, to give you a future and a hope.

1. What previous plans, purposes and dreams have you had?

2. Do you find that they have been set aside? If so how can you stir them up?

<u>Day 3</u>

Hebrews 12:12-13 - Therefore lift your drooping hands and strengthen your weak knees, and make straight paths for your feet, so that what is lame may not be put out of joint but rather be healed.

Hebrews 10:19-23 - Therefore, brothers, since we have confidence to enter the holy places by the blood of Jesus, by the new and living way that he opened for us through the curtain, that is, through his flesh, and since we have a great priest over the house of God, let us draw near with a true heart in full assurance of faith, with our hearts sprinkled clean from an evil conscience and our bodies washed with pure water. Let us hold fast the confession of our hope without wavering, for he who promised is faithful.

1. What do these 2 scriptures say to you about getting out of the daily survival mode?

14

2. What choices can you make today that will allow you to lift the drooping hands and step with confidence out of the fog into what He has called you into?

<u>Day 4</u>

Hebrews 4:16 - Let us then with confidence draw near to the throne of grace, that we may receive mercy and find grace to help in time of need.

Spend time today at the throne of grace. Listen as He speaks and guides you to a new place of walking in His planned destiny for your life.

1. What distractions have allowed for a foggy faded vision in your life?

2. Make steps today to change those distractions.

Day 5

Once we are aware of the fog bank - our daily survival lifestyle of distractions - it allows us the opportunity to stop and reverse. Looking at Jesus and refocusing our life is as easy as hitting the brakes.

I John 4:16-17 - So we have come to know and to believe the love that God has for us. God is love, and whoever abides in love abides in God, and God abides in him. By this is love perfected with us, so that we may have confidence for the day of judgment, because as he is so also are we in this world.

Ps. 103:2-5 - Bless the LORD, O my soul, and forget not all his benefits, who forgives all your iniquity, who heals all your diseases, who redeems your life from the pit, who crowns you with steadfast love and mercy, who satisfies you with good so that your youth is renewed like the eagle's.

1. Where can you stop and refocus?

2. Take time to rejoice in Psalms 103:2-5 above. Journal your thoughts.

Day 6

Re-read *The Fog Veil Was Torn.*

1. Summarize your thoughts about this weeks study?

2. Apply something new today to your personal time with the Lord. (A few suggestions: Sing, Dance, Pray, Read, Take a walk and just talk to Him, Sit in silence just listening.)

   Journal your experience and thoughts of your time spent with the Lord today.

You are blessed and highly favored!

Silencing the Voices of Winter

I find something astonishing about the tiny brilliant colored crocus flowers. They are designed to push up through the ground at a time when all of nature is still asleep. They feel a ray of warmth that most of nature misses and it stirs them to believe for what is true and close at hand.

They are sprinkled for weeks with dustings of snow, chilled by the frosty breath of winds and adorned with frost every morning but they still stand tall proclaiming their internal knowledge of the truth of the emanate arrival of spring.

The crocus's appearance signals within us as well - our knowing that even though the snow still lightly may fall, the wind still blows its chilly breath and the slippery icy frost still awaits our footprints in the morning - the warmth of spring is unfolding. These voices of winter are silenced because we believe in the creator's consistent design of nature.

Within each of us is that spiritual "knowing" of our design as well. Our life situations may not look different – the snows are still falling, the winds are still blowing and the frosty mornings still arrive – but inside is a promise that was fulfilled at the cross for each of us.

Just as the crocus raises its tiny head in colorful victory we too can stand strong in His promise. His promise of complete forgiveness is given as a gift and brings us the strength of the crocus to push back the voices that whisper of our past failures and faults.

His abundant extravagant love poured out doesn't remember any of them.

Look forward with me daily to walking as the crocus – full of expectation of spring's complete work within you.

Day 1

Spend some time contemplating what *Silencing the Voices of Winter* means to you.

1. What does this mean to you?

2. How does it apply to your life?

<u>Day 2</u>

Romans 5:10-11 - For if while we were enemies we were reconciled to God by the death of his Son, much more, now that we are reconciled, shall we be save by his life. More than that, we also rejoice in God through our Lord Jesus Christ, through whom we have now received reconciliation.

Psalm 103:10-12 - He does not deal with us according to our sins, nor repay us according to our iniquities. For as high as the heavens are above the earth, so great is his steadfast love toward those who fear him; as far as the east is from the west, so far does he remove our transgressions from us.

What an awesome assurance. Because of the blood of Christ there is nothing we have done or will do that will ever separate us from His steadfast love. Basking in that realization gives us the strength to move forward into all of Gods abundant promises and purposes. No looking back at the past! If He doesn't hold anything against us – we should not either!

1. Take time today to write down the haunting past transgressions of your life. Now re-read the above scripture and with it in mind shred that paper and throw it away.

21

Day 3

II Corinthians 12:9-10 - But he said to me, "My grace is sufficient for you, for my power is made perfect in weakness." Therefore I will boast all the more gladly of my weaknesses, so that the power of Christ may rest upon me. For the sake of Christ, then, I am content with weaknesses, insults, hardships, persecutions, and calamities. For when I am weak, then I am strong.

We all struggle with life situations. However, knowing that He knows our steps and by walking through them with our eyes focused on Him we are victorious.

1. What life situations – snow, winds and frost – have a discouraging grip on you right now?

2. How can you apply the above scripture to those situations and raise your head in victory through them?

Day 4

The peace of God is a promise that walks us through many of the coldest snowfalls, the strongest windstorms and the frostiest mornings. Living a life of peace comes from knowing the loving hand of our Lord always "has our back". Cultivating a walk of basking in His presence, listening and becoming saturated in that peace is a discipline many never find because of a hectic life. The time to stir that is NOW not in the midst of a crisis.

Isaiah 54:10 - For the mountains may depart and the hills be removed, but my steadfast love shall not depart from you, and my covenant of peace shall not be removed," says the Lord, who has compassion on you.

Lamentations 3:22-23 - The steadfast love of the Lord never ceases; his mercies never come to an end; they are new every morning; great is your faithfulness.

Take time today to sit in quiet - waiting in His presence. Drink in the peace of God. Lay all the life situations down and journal your thoughts about His peace and unfailing love.

Day 5

His extravagant love for us is intoxicating. Living a life steeped in that love drives away the voices of winter – lies of our faults and failures, as well as the difficult situations of life – our snowstorms, windstorms and frosty mornings.

Psalms 36:5-9 - Your steadfast love, O Lord, extends to the heavens, your faithfulness to the clouds. Your righteousness is like the mountains of God; your judgments are like the great deep; man and beast you save, O Lord. How precious is your steadfast love, O God! The children of mankind take refuge in the shadow of your wings. They feast on the abundance of your house, and you give them drink from the river of your delights. For with you is the fountain of life; in your light do we see light.

Song of Solomon 4:7 - You are altogether beautiful, my love; there is no flaw in you.

1. How would you describe your understanding of Christ's unconditional love for you personally?

2. The above scripture speaks of no flaw in you – Take time today to write down at least 5 things that are GREAT about yourself. Rejoice in HIS creative forces that designed you to be exactly who you are.

Day 6

Re-read *Silencing the Voices of Winter*.

1. What discouraging situations have you been able to gain victory over this week, as you placed them under the blood of Christ and cultivated a lifestyle of basking in His peace?

2. Spend some time today in thankfulness for His extravagant love, grace, and peace through Jesus Christ.

You are Victorious!

Step Over the Threshold or Slam the Door

Just as the flowering trees of spring signal that spring is arriving; so do your life experiences create your personal life paradigm.

This life paradigm is one that says, "When I see this" - "this is the result".

Your need to "see it" to "believe it" isn't something new to society, it's the same innate thinking that Jesus saw as He taught the multitudes.

At the lake of Gennesaret after a long night of fishing, the natural in Peter questioned Jesus when He told him to let his nets down again for a catch. However, Peter chose to say, "Yes". His response allowed Jesus to perform a miracle that was witnessed by him and many others.

To the multitudes amazement they "saw it" – a catch so large that it took two boats to the brink of sinking. They knew this was not a natural experience.

To Peter it triggered a faith eruption, seeing beyond his life paradigm and it became a life-altering experience. He left what he knew and followed Jesus.

So my question has been, why did Jesus do that?

27

I believe He knew all the fears and accusations Peter would experience in years to come and Jesus gave Peter a "see it" to "believe it" moment to draw a line in the sand for him. Here was a moment in time for him to remember – a place to stand and push back the lies, fears and accusations that would come to whisper in his ear.

The plan for His life unfolded the day he chose to follow Jesus and leave his nets. However, the life he entered held many obstacles and the catch of fish that one eventful day opened his eyes to who Jesus was.

We all live with decisions made or not made, and with regrets that can whisper for years in our ears.

The silencing of those lies, accusations and fears was done for us at the cross of Jesus. If we make the choice to look only at the face of Jesus and His poured out love that was given to us undeserved; then we can stand victorious against those lies, fears and accusations, and move into the great plans and purposes that we are designed for.

We too, experience by the Holy Spirits direction things that defy our life paradigm and we too, must make a choice to step over the threshold and through that door believing or slam the door in disbelief.

These decisions can be life-altering experiences for us.

They can lead us to see who Jesus is and bring us to a fulfilling purpose or they can keep us in a life that lives continually in the "see it" to "believe it" cycle of existence.

My choice is to walk in a new paradigm, one that is God designed – "He promised it so I believe it".

Day 1

Spend some time contemplating what _Step Over the Threshold or Slam the Door_ means to you.

1. What does this mean to you?

2. How does it apply to your life?

Day 2

Luke 5:1-10 - On one occasion, while the crowd was pressing in on him to hear the word of God, he was standing by the lake of Gennesaret, and he saw two boats by the lake, but the fishermen had gone out of them and were washing their nets. Getting into one of the boats, which was Simon's, he asked him to put out a little from the land. And he sat down and taught the people from the boat. And when he had finished speaking, he said to Simon, "Put out into the deep and let down your nets for a catch." And Simon answered, "Master, we toiled all night and took nothing! But at your word I will let down the nets." And when they had done this, they enclosed a large number of fish, and their nets were breaking. They signaled to their partners in the other boat to come and help them. And they came and filled both the boats, so that they began to sink. But when Simon Peter saw it, he fell down at Jesus' knees, saying, "Depart from me, for I am a sinful man, O Lord." For he and all who were with him were astonished at the catch of fish that they had taken,

At different times of our lives we all walk in a "See it" to "Believe it" place.

The Holy Spirit woos us by placing reminders of his presence in very real situations. Such as the time you worried about feeding your children and unexpected funds come in the mail, a phone call from a good friend right when you were at the breaking point, etc. Our paradigm regarding these events shapes our faith.

1. In what area of your life right now are you at a "See it" to "Believe it" place?

2. Think of times that you have experienced the Holy Spirits wooing. Describe those experiences and how you felt.

<u>Day 3</u>

Hebrews 11:1 - Now faith is the assurance of things hoped for, the conviction of things not seen.

Ephesians 1:15-18 - For this reason, because I have heard of your faith in the Lord Jesus and your love toward all the saints, I do not cease to give thanks for you, remembering you in my prayers, that the God of our Lord Jesus Christ, the Father of glory, may give you the Spirit of wisdom and of revelation in the knowledge of him, having the eyes of your hearts enlightened, that you may know what is the hope to which he has called you, what are the riches of his glorious inheritance in the saints.

1. What does it mean to you to have the eyes of your heart enlightened?

2. Conviction is a deep internal "knowing". Is your faith based on that type of "knowing" or do you tend toward explaining away the God encounters of your life – slamming the door?

3. We can't decide to change our life paradigm but the unconditional love of Christ can. However, how we accept the unexpected - sometimes unusual - things that "walk" into our lives can allow the "line drawn in the sand" life altering experiences that can change us. Take time today to consider these thoughts.

Day 4

Isaiah 43:10-11 - "You are my witnesses," declares the Lord, "and my servant whom I have chosen, that you may know and believe me and understand that I am he. Before me no god was formed, nor shall there be any after me. I, I am the Lord, and besides me there is no savior.

Romans 8:38-39 - For I am sure that neither death nor life, nor angels nor rulers, nor things present nor things to come, nor powers, nor height nor depth, nor anything else in all creation, will be able to separate us from the love of God in Christ Jesus our Lord.

1. Peter experienced a "God encounter" when Jesus provided a miraculous catch of fish and his response was to acknowledge the deity of Christ, thus changing his life forever. Our understanding of the two scriptures above can do the same today. Journal your thoughts.

Spend some time today to "be still" before Him and listen as you contemplate these scriptures.

Day 5

Ephesians 2:10 - For we are his workmanship, created in Christ Jesus for good works, which God prepared beforehand, that we should walk in them.

Psalm 8:1-9 - O Lord, our Lord, how majestic is your name in all the earth! You have set your glory above the heavens. Out of the mouth of babies and infants, you have established strength because of your foes, to still the enemy and the avenger. When I look at your heavens, the work of your fingers, the moon and the stars, which you have set in place, what is man that you are mindful of him, and the son of man that you care for him? Yet you have made him a little lower than the heavenly beings and crowned him with glory and honor. You have given him dominion over the works of your hands; you have put all things under his feet, all sheep and oxen, and also the beasts of the field, the birds of the heavens, and the fish of the sea, whatever passes along the paths of the seas. O Lord, our Lord, how majestic is your name in all the earth!

   Peter's experience with the miraculous catch of fish caused a life altering change in him. He moved into a new lifestyle and changed the history of the church.

We too can move into a lifestyle where the abundant favor and direction of the Holy Spirit will direct our plans and purposes - which will bring us greater joy then anything we can do on our own.

1. What would it mean to you to "step over the threshold" into a lifestyle directed by the Holy Spirits voice?

2. How can you apply that today?

<u>Day 6</u>

Re-read *Step Over the Threshold or Slam the Door.*

    1. How has your life paradigm changed this week?

    2. Do you have a "line drawn in the sand" encounter to strengthen your convictions?

    3. Journal any thoughts that the Holy Spirit stirred as you re-read this weeks prose.

You are redeemed!

Creations Explosion of New Life and Promise!

As we feel, smell and hear spring approaching it stirs and renews something inside of our very being. It's a promise of new life that is ignited by the very emergence of the small internal voice saying "YES" and "Amen" to the creators promise.

There is a perpetual movement within nature that precedes spring.

Weeks before, temperatures begin to warm. The signaling begins the onset of spring and something begins to stir in all of creation. It's a belief, a faith that has been placed deep inside of her. That faith is that New Life is possible and is coming.

With that begins a stirring and a movement that grows within the very sap of the trees, the hull of the seeds, the growing creation within the eggs and the wombs of the unborn animals; it is the YES and AMEN of creation to the creators promise of new life.

Once the time has come - the eruption begins its song as the buds of trees and flowers burst into bloom. Seeds dormant under the earth now explode into life while birds of all species and sizes begin the process of their hatching. They begin the pecking and cracking open of their protective shell, and the birthing process of animals all around us begins to burst forth with the sounds of new life.

All of nature sings forth with conformation of that internal voice of faith in His promises.

We too, with anticipation of spring's creative explosion see promise and new life around our lives.

His plan is always for you!   His plan is for promise and new life in your family, your job, your physical being etc.

Join me today as we say YES and AMEN to His promises for our lives.

Day 1

Spend some time contemplating what *Creations Explosion of New Life and Promise!* means to you.

1. What does this mean to you?

2. How does it apply to your life?

<u>Day 2</u>

II Peter 1:3-4 - His divine power has granted to us all things that pertain to life and godliness, through the knowledge of him who called us to his own glory and excellence, by which he has granted to us his precious and very great promises, so that through them you may become partakers of the divine nature, having escaped from the corruption that is in the world because of sinful desire.

1. Through Christ we have been given power and all the promises of God. How would you describe the above scripture working in your life?

2. Spend time in His presence today contemplating and journaling your thoughts regarding His divine power, promises and divine nature all given to us at the cross.

Day 3

II Corinthians 1:20 – For all the promises of God find their Yes in him. That is why it is through him that we utter our Amen to God for his glory.

> 1. This scripture is a great revelation as to what belongs to the heirs of the Kingdom of God. We, as children have access to ALL of His promises. Spend some time today in the Bible searching out many of the promises. Take a few minutes and journal your favorite ones that pertain to your life right now.

Day 4

Colossians 1:15-20 - He is the image of the invisible God, the firstborn of all creation. For by him all things were created, in heaven and on earth, visible and invisible, whether thrones or dominions or rulers or authorities—all things were created through him and for him. And he is before all things, and in him all things hold together. And he is the head of the body, the church. He is the beginning, the firstborn from the dead, that in everything he might be preeminent. For in him all the fullness of God was pleased to dwell, and through him to reconcile to himself all things, whether on earth or in heaven, making peace by the blood of his cross.

1. New Life is only possible because of the cross of Christ. Our dormant life was redeemed and now has the possibility of new life. Just as trees, flowers and seeds burst open with the knowledge of Christ's redemption we too can become all that was infused into us. What possibilities within you are stirring and ready to burst out?

2. How can you stir them today?

3. Being still before the Lord will bring peace and will allow the voice of the Holy Spirit to stir forgotten desires and directions. Take time today to be still before Him. Journal your thoughts from that time.

Day 5

Psalm 19:1 - The heavens declare the glory of God, and the sky above proclaims his handiwork.

I Corinthians 14:15 - What am I to do? I will pray with my spirit, but I will pray with my mind also; I will sing praise with my spirit, but I will sing with my mind also.

Psalm 47:1 - Clap your hands, all peoples! Shout to God with loud songs of joy!

1. The sounds of spring are ones of rejoicing. The above scriptures express how we can rejoice. What are you filled with rejoicing for today?

2. Spend time today declaring the faithfulness of God either by journaling, in prayer or in song.

<u>Day 6</u>

Re-read *<u>Creations Explosion of New Life and Promise!</u>*

1. What new revelation from God did you receive this week as you spent time in His presence?

2. Can you apply this directly to your daily life? If so - where?

You are an heir to the KINGDOM!

Ready to Run Before the Wind

As a sailboat with an unbalanced load will list and drift off its course, often a similar drifting time can occur in your life.

Questions, pain and loneliness begin to flow in and out. Faith anchors you to a deep stillness and contentment within that ultimately will prevail.

Staying the storm, waiting for the wind to stir and purposefully setting about trimming and rebalancing the load takes a dependence on the knowledge of His plans and purposes for your life.

Your faith and understanding of who you are as an heir in the Kingdom is your strength and anchor.

Timing in the process is crucial. A turn in direction made to quickly will cause disaster, ending in pulling you out of the wind and the ultimate possibility of capsize or luffing - no wind in the sails or desire for it.

The Lord keeps you in a safe harbor - keeping you safe from all attack as time and preparation work within you. As you rest in this safe harbor the turning process begins.

This place of preparation allows you to trim your sails, adjusting them to allow maximum efficiency as the sails become "Full".

The fullness of your sails will bring you to a healthy place of "getting on with the job" that He has placed before you.

This fullness will allow this job it to be done in a steady relaxed way, without stress and urgency.

Just as a sailboat begins to "come about", the turning begins ever so slightly as each wave is taking you toward a new direction, allowing momentum to carry you forward.

This time of turning is often a lonely difficult place. However, it will direct you into an awareness that will slowly surge within and stir anticipation for the coming process. At the appropriate time you will begin to cry out for what is to come.

You will come to a new place where with sails trimmed and full you will be propelled forward into new waters - ready to run before the wind.

The adventure ahead will be one of full sails, movement and new horizons. You will see new places in the spirit and be moved to heights of effectiveness that you have never imagined.

As the stillness begins to change, you can feel the beginning of a breeze. With a breath that quivers within and the surge of movement – the rise of a wave begins to break.

"It is time, it is time, it is time!
Catch it now!
Run before the wind!"

The waves begin to respond to the breeze as they rise and fall. The sails begin to breath in and out just as your spirit begins to anticipate the coming movement.

Don't hold back.

Feel the freedom that comes with the movement. Step into the call He has placed within you.

Now is the time to sail forward being propelled into all that He has purposed and prepared for you.

You are ready to run before the wind.

NOTE: (To help those of us who are not nautical in our understanding the following are for better clarity of the above prose.)

My understanding of the following sailing terms:

"Full" sails = getting on with the job but in a steady relaxed way, without undue urgency or strain.

Listing = leaning and drifting

Trimming the sails = adjustment needed to improve balance and bring maximum efficiency.

Unbalanced load = Is a defect needing correction

Tacking / heeling = changing direction

<u>Coming about</u> = the momentum that carries the vessel forward.

<u>Luffing</u>= no wind in the sail

<u>Running downwind (Running before the wind)</u> = wind directly behind you moving you forward.

<u>Day 1</u>

Spend some time contemplating what _Ready to Run Before the Wind_ means to you.

1. What does this mean to you?

2. How does it apply to your life?

Day 2

Ready to Run Before the Wind speaks of a process that we can find ourselves in many times in our lives. That process is one of holding onto our faith, listening intently to the voice of God, waiting in safe harbors, preparation and movement into new places. Each piece of the above process has a specific place and can't be "short circuited" without causing possible capsize. Wherever you find yourself today in this process – embrace it. Be content in your walk and allow your faith to do its perfect work.

Galatians 2:20 - I have been crucified with Christ. It is no longer I who live, but Christ who lives in me. And the life I now live in the flesh I live by faith in the Son of God, who loved me and gave himself for me.

Hebrews 6:17-20 - So when God desired to show more convincingly to the heirs of the promise the unchangeable character of his purpose, he guaranteed it with an oath, so that by two unchangeable things, in which it is impossible for God to lie, we who have fled for refuge might have strong encouragement to hold fast to the hope set before us.

We have this as a sure and steadfast anchor of the soul, a hope that enters into the inner place behind the curtain, where Jesus has gone as a forerunner on our behalf, having become a high priest forever after the order of Melchizedek.

1. In the above process, where do you find yourself today?

2. When your life gets "stormy" what is your anchor? How can you express your faith and with contentment walk forward during those times?

<u>Day 3</u>

Listening to the voice of God and His direction is crucial in your time of decisions. Heeding instructions such as "Do this, Go here, etc" can be the difference between a peaceful "sailing" or a lengthy frustrated "stormy" situation. Hearing His voice over the clang of many friends' opinions is a learning process as well. My telltale answer is always asking myself the simple question "is there peace in this decision?" If confusion is there - don't do it.

II Corinthians 3:17 - Now the Lord is the Spirit, and where the Spirit of the Lord is, there is freedom.

John 16:13 - When the Spirit of truth comes, he will guide you into all the truth, for he will not speak on his own authority, but whatever he hears he will speak, and he will declare to you the things that are to come.

1. In the learning process we all make decisions both ways – on our own thoughts and hearing Gods voice. Contemplate decisions you have made both ways and what were the results?

2. Do you have decisions you currently are in the middle of? How can you apply a lifestyle of listening to His voice - Thus, resulting in results of peace?

Day 4

If we are anchored to our faith and learn to hear the voice of God, where our journey leads us He promises us "safe harbor" – one of peace. This place in the process requires patience. Waiting for His direction and movement has to come from a place of peace. If struggle begins it becomes about you not Him. Sitting and waiting in His presence is all about just that – sitting and waiting – focus on His face, His presence and nothing about what you can or can't do. Often, as this time progresses this can be one of hearing His voice clearly and direction for the coming movement will begin to stir within your heart.

Psalm 17:5-8 - My steps have held fast to your paths; my feet have not slipped. I call upon you, for you will answer me, O God; incline your ear to me; hear my words. Wondrously show your steadfast love, O Savior of those who seek refuge from their adversaries at your right hand. Keep me as the apple of your eye; hide me in the shadow of your wings,

Psalm 91:1-2 - He who dwells in the shelter of the Most High will abide in the shadow of the Almighty. I will say to the Lord, "My refuge and my fortress, my God, in whom I trust."

1. You can find yourself at the beginning of this "safe harbor" or nearing the approach of "new wind" and movement coming. Which place are you in?

2. How do you know?

3. How can you apply this place to a place of contentment - walking in His plans and purposes for you right now?

Day 5

I Thessalonians 1:4 - For we know, brothers loved by God, that he has chosen you,

Psalm 37:23-24 - The steps of a man are established by the Lord, when he delights in his way; though he fall, he shall not be cast headlong, for the Lord upholds his hand.

1. Where do you feel preparation for movement beginning to stir?

2. What has He chosen you for?

Day 6

Re-read *Ready to Run Before the Wind*.

1. What dreams, plans and purposes have you had that have been stirred up this week?

2. Taking into consideration where you find yourself at in the "sailing" process - take time today to re-evaluate those dreams. Allow the Holy Spirit to stir and redirect you into His purposes.

You are His Chosen Child!

The Beauty of First Flight – Believe You Are Made For More!

The butterfly's journey begins long before her first flight. Starting with the caterpillar that doesn't comprehend that a transformation waits ahead. Its hunger pushes it forward foraging for life-giving sustenance that will allow the strength for the formation of a freshly spun place of private metamorphosis. Upon arrival in this cocoon the process begins. It is the time to rest, to wait, to trust in the creators plan. The transformation that transpires while sealed in this cocoon is remarkable. It allows a creation that was made to crawl find its wings to fly. Soon the cocoon opens and releases this new beauty. She comes forth - unfurls her wings and RESTS in the SUN, here waiting for the strength to lift her new found wings and take her first flight.

Finally anticipation swells within and as gentle as a breath she lifts up upon those paper thin wings and launches into a new life that now involves new heights and new horizons that could never have been achieved without this transformation.

The willingness to *"Be Still and Know that I Am God"* is that process of metamorphosis that allows the caterpillar to become the butterfly.

It will also allow a transformation in your life that will take you from one who strives to one who trusts completely in your Lord.

The thought process of "work to **achieve** all that there is to success" is exchanged for one that "**believes** you are made for more".

You can REST in the SON for His release, His direction and His wind of abundance that will be blown beneath newfound wings that are ready to launch into a life that involves new heights and new visions.

Your anticipation will swell inside as the wind and the spirit come beneath your wings to carry you higher and further then you could have gone by your own work as the caterpillar.

Believe you are made for more and take that first flight of "Being Still and Knowing that He is God"!

Day 1

Spend some time contemplating what *The Beauty of First Flight – Believe You Are Made For More!* means to you.

1. What does this mean to you?

2. How does it apply to your life?

Day 2

Romans 5:1-5 - Therefore, since we have been justified by faith, we have peace with God through our Lord Jesus Christ. Through him we have also obtained access by faith into this grace in which we stand, and we rejoice in hope of the glory of God. Not only that, but we rejoice in our sufferings, knowing that suffering produces endurance, and endurance produces character, and character produces hope, and hope does not put us to shame, because God's love has been poured into our hearts through the Holy Spirit who has been given to us.

1. Does your faith continue to push you forward as the caterpillar – foraging for life giving sustenance or are you satisfied to stay where you are?

2. How can you use the above scripture to encourage your forward movement?

Day 3

Trusting in His plan of transformation in your life will bring peace and assurance to your heart. His plans for you are always ones of FAVOR and BLESSING. Allowing His cocooning process allows you to spin out all the business and distractions of your life to become one who looks only to the Son.

II Corinthians 4:16-18 - So we do not lose heart. Though our outer self is wasting away, our inner self is being renewed day by day. For this light momentary affliction is preparing for us an eternal weight of glory beyond all comparison, as we look not to the things that are seen but to the things that are unseen. For the things that are seen are transient, but the things that are unseen are eternal.

1. Spend time today journaling your thoughts regarding yesterday and today's' scriptures - Romans 5:1-5 and II Corinthians 4:16-18?

Day 4

Our lives are ones filled with the anxiety of daily survival. Just as Martha was troubled about getting everything done and the unfairness of Mary's decision to sit at the Lord's feet - so do many things that aren't important bother us. When we re-focus our eyes to the unfailing unconditional love and assurance of Christ all the daily survival issues seem to melt away.

Luke 10:41-42 - But the Lord answered her, "Martha, Martha, you are anxious and troubled about many things, but one thing is necessary. Mary has chosen the good portion, which will not be taken away from her."

PS. 138:8 - The LORD will fulfill his purpose for me; your steadfast love, O LORD, endures forever.....

1. During this study have you been able to see the distractions of daily survival issues?

2. List some of those and how you can change their impact as a distraction on your life?

Day 5

Philippians 4:13 - I can do all things through him who strengthens me.

Psalm 46:10 - "Be still, and know that I am God. I will be exalted among the nations, I will be exalted in the earth!"

1. How can embracing these two scriptures help as you adjust your life to one of RESTING, WAITING and PEACE in His presence?

2. Take time to Rest, Wait and Listen to the Holy Spirit today. Journal your thoughts.

Day 6

Re-read *The Beauty of First Flight – Believe You Are Made For More!.*

1. What do you see in your future as you contemplate the wings that He is developing in your life and the new dreams and purposes? Spend time contemplating what those look like.

2. What new thoughts about your uniqueness have been stirred this week?

3. Take quiet time today to just sit in the Presence of our King. Listen to His voice and allow a thankful heart to stir a desire for the transformation completion and what your first flight as a butterfly will look like.

You are a NEW Creation!

Be Who You Were Created To Be

A well-known slogan often rings in our ears, "Be all you can be", but we were created to be exactly who we are. We already are all we can be if we acknowledge and walk in that assurance.

The Fathers original design in nature expresses itself to us again in the simple concept of being who you were created to BE. Nature knows that which it is created to be and it just IS!

Grapes grow grapes; even when grafted, they still produce grapes not flowers. An apple tree knows within its design what it is to produce; trying to produce an orange just won't work. Birds, Fish and animals all pro—create from their own kind. They just know instinctively who they are and it's easy; it's natural and peace reigns. No working, researching, studying required; they KNOW how to BE!

We humans on the other hand try so hard to BE better, BE happier, BE different, or BE someone else.

If we can learn to rest and BE at peace with who we are and what we were created to BE, our purpose will present itself and will bring us fulfillment and peace. Fruit will be automatic; we will just Be!

Many times we may require 40 years in the wilderness of TRY, TRY, TRY before we come to a place where we can stop, look around and see what it means to just BE!

The key we must find is GOD; not rules, regulations, TO DO's and DO NOT's but meeting HIM face to face. HIS presence brings that understanding and will change you.

Living in the place of HIS presence, hearing HIS voice and tapping into the chemistry within makes you WHO you are. Knowing who you are will bring a freedom of knowing how to BE.

That freedom will reveal the chemistry that ONLY you were designed with. ONLY your unique thoughts, abilities, gifts, and personality where made with HIS purpose in mind. Your very DNA - unique ONLY to you can produce the specific fruit that HE planned. NO trying is involved. Just BE and walk in that confidence that YOU already are ALL YOU can BE.

<u>Day 1</u>

Spend some time contemplating what <u>*Be Who You Were Created To Be!*</u> means to you.

1. What does this mean to you?

2. How does it apply to your life?

Day 2

Romans 5: 1-2 - Therefore, since we have been justified by faith, we have peace with God through our Lord Jesus Christ. Through him we have also obtained access by faith into this grace in which we stand, and we rejoice in hope of the glory of God

Galatians 5:6 - For in Christ Jesus neither circumcision nor uncircumcision counts for anything, but only faith working through love.

Being who we are created to be requires a place of contentment and peace at our core. That peace and contentment comes from faith and knowing that we are loved. Nothing we can do or do not do changes that love.

1. Have you found yourself in the TRYING to BE someone or something that you just can't be?

2. List a few of those times you have found yourself in that position and how you felt, as well as end results.

3. If you are in that struggle right now contemplate the above two scriptures and make a choice to BE who you are not what the struggle of life is asking of you.

Day 3

We are all designed to BE who God created us to BE – in our very DNA we have traits and gifts He chose just for us. Finding peace with who you are allows those gifts to surface. You find your place of understanding those gifts at the feet of Jesus. His presence and voice will direct you into all that He has planned for your life.

James 1:17 - Every good gift and every perfect gift is from above, coming down from the Father of lights with whom there is no variation or shadow due to change.

I Peter 2:16 - Live as people who are free, not using your freedom as a cover-up for evil, but living as servants of God.

1. What traits and gifts do you see differently through the above scriptures?

2. Take time today to sit in His presence and listen to His voice about who you are created to BE. Journal your thoughts.

Day 4

Being given an assignment from our heavenly Father is an awesome thought. All of who we are created to BE was programmed into us to fulfill each of those assignments. What's yours?

If we take time to look at each of the disciples - they each had specific talents, gifts and directions. We too may have different assignments in life and in the kingdom of God throughout the seasons of our life.

I Corinthians 7:17-24 - Only let each person lead the life that the Lord has assigned to him, and to which God has called him. This is my rule in all the churches. Was anyone at the time of his call already circumcised? Let him not seek to remove the marks of circumcision. Was anyone at the time of his call uncircumcised? Let him not seek circumcision. For neither circumcision counts for anything nor uncircumcision, but keeping the commandments of God. Each one should remain in the condition in which he was called. Were you a bondservant when called? Do not be concerned about it. (But if you can gain your freedom, avail yourself of the opportunity.) For he who was called in the Lord as a bondservant is a freedman of the Lord. Likewise he who was free when called is a bondservant of Christ. You were bought with a price; do not become bondservants of men.

So, brothers, in whatever condition each was called, there let him remain with God.

II Corinthians 10:13 - But we will not boast beyond limits, but will boast only with regard to the area of influence God assigned to us, to reach even to you.

1. What assignments – use of natural talents and gifts, acquired learned talents and gifts as well as God directed favor and opened doors – do you see currently active in your life?

Day 5

Romans 12:6-8 - Having gifts that differ according to the grace given to us, let us use them: if prophecy, in proportion to our faith; if service, in our serving; the one who teaches, in his teaching; the one who exhorts, in his exhortation; the one who contributes, in generosity; the one who leads, with zeal; the one who does acts of mercy, with cheerfulness.

Proverbs 18:16 - A man's gift makes room for him and brings him before the great.

1. Humility – a true understanding of who you are – makes room for you. Have you seen this operating in your life?

2. Of the few spiritual gifts listed in Romans 12:6-8 which do you feel are working in your life? And why? What others – not listed – are part of who you are?

3. Spend time in His presence today listening for direction and possible new assignments.

Day 6

Re-read *Be Who You Were Created To Be!*.

Matthew 5:14-16 - "You are the light of the world. A city set on a hill cannot be hidden. Nor do people light a lamp and put it under a basket, but on a stand, and it gives light to all in the house. In the same way, let your light shine before others, so that they may see your good works and give glory to your Father who is in heaven.

1. What revelations have you received this week about who you were created to BE?

2. Journal your thoughts and directions.

You are created in His image!

Life Giving Presence – The River

The parallels of nature and spiritual intrigue me as I contemplate our lives and our need for strength, support and relationships that often come from connecting with a body of people who believe as we do. The church, with all her faults just happens to be that body.

Just as a drop of water that is entombed in a dark cloud anticipates release into the small beckoning spring below, so are we. This raindrops release unites it with the refreshing spring as it becomes one with the forming "rivlets". These flow in turn in a steady motion forward marching toward the stream of living water that is bubbling and greeting them from below.

As they merge into this stream they grow in strength and speed seeking out and forming ways to reach the next goal of uniting with a wider, deeper and more forceful body called The River.

The River has an identity of its own! Joining with this body the anticipation grows overwhelming. The purpose as part of this river will be to bring life to all that grows on its banks and to all that inhabits its depths. The speed, force, depth and width of this amazing river changes as each stream enters.

The river creates its own path even breaking into new areas and over barriers of rock allowing the formation of cascading falls that refresh previously barren and dry land. This Rivers very existence draws creation to its banks for the life giving presence it provides. This water brings refreshment and life, strengthening all that lives within its presence, changing the very atmosphere.

As nature parallels the spiritual so are we as that drop of water. Once we find The River – a body of believers - that brings life to us, so sets our purpose.

Seek the presence and face of Jesus that will give you strength and life and a River where you can grow and be part of changing the very atmosphere around you.

Day 1

Spend some time contemplating what _Life Giving Presence – The River_ means to you.

1. What does this mean to you?

2. How does it apply to your life?

Day 2

As individuals that have accepted the gift of Christ's sacrifice we have been given a gift of adoption into the kingdom of God. You - that single drop are part of the entire "ocean". Your decision to step out of the "single drop" mentality into a river – a church body - is made with many differing stipulations – all of which are as unique as you are. However, one thing is the same. Your eyes are focused on the lover of your soul.

Psalm 147:3-11 - He heals the brokenhearted and binds up their wounds. He determines the number of the stars; he gives to all of them their names. Great is our Lord, and abundant in power; his understanding is beyond measure. The Lord lifts up the humble; he casts the wicked to the ground. Sing to the Lord with thanksgiving; make melody to our God on the lyre! He covers the heavens with clouds; he prepares rain for the earth; he makes grass grow on the hills. He gives to the beasts their food, and to the young ravens that cry. His delight is not in the strength of the horse, nor his pleasure in the legs of a man, but the Lord takes pleasure in those who fear him, in those who hope in his steadfast love.

1. Spend time today journaling your thoughts regarding your hope in His steadfast love for you.

Day 3

As we begin the transition from "single drop" mentality to desiring more, the presence of the Holy Spirit will draw us deeper into this process.

Psalm 42:1 - As a deer pants for flowing streams, so pants my soul for you, O God.

Isaiah 35:6 - then shall the lame man leap like a deer, and the tongue of the mute sing for joy. For waters break forth in the wilderness, and streams in the desert;

1. Do you desire a deeper place in experiencing the presence of God, more understanding of the Bible and more connection to others with like minds?

2. Have you reached out to connect with other believers? If not, why?

3. Express your desire for a deeper place.

Day 4

II Peter 1:16-21 - For we did not follow cleverly devised myths when we made known to you the power and coming of our Lord Jesus Christ, but we were eyewitnesses of his majesty. For when he received honor and glory from God the Father, and the voice was borne to him by the Majestic Glory, "This is my beloved Son, with whom I am well pleased," we ourselves heard this very voice borne from heaven, for we were with him on the holy mountain. And we have the prophetic word more fully confirmed, to which you will do well to pay attention as to a lamp shining in a dark place, until the day dawns and the morning star rises in your hearts, knowing this first of all, that no prophecy of Scripture comes from someone's own interpretation. For no prophecy was ever produced by the will of man, but men spoke from God as they were carried along by the Holy Spirit.

Isaiah 61: 1-11 - The Spirit of the Lord God is upon me, because the Lord has anointed me to bring good news to the poor; he has sent me to bind up the brokenhearted, to proclaim liberty to the captives, and the opening of the prison to those who are bound; to proclaim the year of the Lord's favor, and the day of vengeance of our God; to comfort all who mourn;

to grant to those who mourn in Zion—to give them a beautiful headdress instead of ashes, the oil of gladness instead of mourning, the garment of praise instead of a faint spirit; that they may be called oaks of righteousness, the planting of the Lord, that he may be glorified. They shall build up the ancient ruins; they shall raise up the former devastations; they shall repair the ruined cities, the devastations of many generations. Strangers shall stand and tend your flocks; foreigners shall be your plowmen and vinedressers; but you shall be called the priests of the Lord; they shall speak of you as the ministers of our God; you shall eat the wealth of the nations, and in their glory you shall boast. Instead of your shame there shall be a double portion; instead of dishonor they shall rejoice in their lot; therefore in their land they shall possess a double portion; they shall have everlasting joy. For I the Lord love justice; I hate robbery and wrong; I will faithfully give them their recompense, and I will make an everlasting covenant with them. Their offspring shall be known among the nations, and their descendants in the midst of the peoples; all who see them shall acknowledge them, that they are an offspring the Lord has blessed. I will greatly rejoice in the Lord; my soul shall exult in my God, for he has clothed me with the garments of salvation; he has covered me with the robe of righteousness, as a bridegroom decks himself like a priest with a beautiful headdress, and as a bride adorns herself with her jewels.

For as the earth brings forth its sprouts, and as a garden causes what is sown in it to sprout up, so the Lord God will cause righteousness and praise to sprout up before all the nations.

1. Relate these two scriptures with your understanding of a church body.

2. Contemplate God's plan regarding your placement in a local church. Journal your thoughts.

Day 5

Ezekiel 47:1-12 - Then he brought me back to the door of the temple, and behold, water was issuing from below the threshold of the temple toward the east (for the temple faced east). The water was flowing down from below the south end of the threshold of the temple, south of the altar. Then he brought me out by way of the north gate and led me around on the outside to the outer gate that faces toward the east; and behold, the water was trickling out on the south side. Going on eastward with a measuring line in his hand, the man measured a thousand cubits, and then led me through the water, and it was ankle-deep. Again he measured a thousand, and led me through the water, and it was knee-deep. Again he measured a thousand, and led me through the water, and it was waist-deep. Again he measured a thousand, and it was a river that I could not pass through, for the water had risen. It was deep enough to swim in, a river that could not be passed through. And he said to me, "Son of man, have you seen this?" Then he led me back to the bank of the river. As I went back, I saw on the bank of the river very many trees on the one side and on the other. And he said to me, "This water flows toward the eastern region and goes down into the Arabah, and enters the sea; when the water flows into the sea, the water will become fresh.

And wherever the river goes, every living creature that swarms will live, and there will be very many fish. For this water goes there, that the waters of the sea may become fresh; so everything will live where the river goes. Fishermen will stand beside the sea. From Engedi to Eneglaim it will be a place for the spreading of nets. Its fish will be of very many kinds, like the fish of the Great Sea. But its swamps and marshes will not become fresh; they are to be left for salt. And on the banks, on both sides of the river, there will grow all kinds of trees for food. Their leaves will not wither, nor their fruit fail, but they will bear fresh fruit every month, because the water for them flows from the sanctuary. Their fruit will be for food, and their leaves for healing."

What an amazing explanation of what the church body – as a river – is intended to be.

1. Do you see the church you are part of - demonstrated in this scripture?

2. Do feel "plugged in" to your local church? If not how can you make a choice to merge your "single drop" into the river?

3. If you don't have a church body that you know God has directed you to, what steps can you make to find one?

Spring's Assurance

<u>Day 6</u>

Re-read <u>*Life Giving Presence – The River.*</u>

Isaiah 52:7 - How beautiful upon the mountains are the feet of him who brings good news, who publishes peace, who brings good news of happiness, who publishes salvation, who says to Zion, "Your God reigns."

Psalm 46:4 -There is a river whose streams make glad the city of God, the holy habitation of the Most High.

As the body of Christ – His Bride – our feet should be seen as beautiful, bringing peace; our mouth one that speaks only love and our lives should pour out streams that make glad those we come in contact with. Being involved with a "presence of God" oriented body of believers you will be changed, refreshed and strengthened to step into assignments that only you are created for and you will see the very atmosphere around you begin to change.

1. Take time today to sit in His presence, rest and listen as He directs your every step.

You are His Beloved!

Mission - Possible

"Your mission if you choose to accept it". These words you all know from popular entertainment but let's consider them in a spiritual sense.

You make a choice to step into many activities in your life. Whether it is at church, work or in extracurricular activities, you find yourself in the impossible situation of "fitting".

How you act, speak and relate to people in those arenas are all connected to that "fitting" process.

Many of them are necessary and many are chosen; but when you honestly evaluate this process you may find it is just plain hard work. What in reality you are doing is trying to fit a round peg into a square hole; it's just not possible.

But "fitting" isn't what you as the "Bride of Christ" are asked to do. In fact it is the exact opposite. Your face and focus needs to be totally on the face of Christ.

You are different and are as a single flower amidst the shrubs. The "fitting" mentality is all about "us" not "Him". The "Him" assignment (mission) focus means that He directs your decisions and your involvement in all areas of your life.

It means your current road will become narrow, directed and more fulfilling because He knows the plans and purposes that your life was designed for.

He has the place that is exactly designed for his single flower to be placed.

The "Him" focus turns your eyes off of your "fitting". You stop and simply ask, "What is my assignment (my mission)?

That assignment can be for an hour, a day, a year or a lifetime. Your part is to ask, choose to accept it and do it. It's not going to be about you but what He has chosen for you to do and in it you will find pure joy.

Living your life in this manner means accepting those assignments whether you "think" you can accomplish them or not.

His assignments often seem impossible to you; but when He gives you a "mission impossible" assignment then you can believe that <u>He will make it possible</u>.

Join me to lay down the "fitting" process. Step out and allow your road to become narrow. Accept the impossible assignments that the Holy Spirit is stirring inside of you and let Him make the impossible possible.

<u>Day 1</u>

Spend some time contemplating what *Mission Possible* means to you.

1. What does this mean to you?

2. How does it apply to your life?

<u>Day 2</u>

The assurance of His steadfast love always opens doors and our eyes to new paths.

Proverbs 3:3-6 - Let not steadfast love and faithfulness forsake you; bind them around your neck; write them on the tablet of your heart. So you will find favor and good success in the sight of God and man. Trust in the Lord with all your heart, and do not lean on your own understanding. In all your ways acknowledge him, and he will make straight your paths.

> 1. How would you describe His faithfulness and steadfast love that He has written on the tablet of your heart"?

Day 3

Stepping on to a narrow path where His presence, voice and direction are primary in your life brings a joy that is often beyond what words can express.

Psalm 16:11 - You make known to me the path of life; in your presence there is fullness of Joy; at your right hand are pleasures forevermore.

1. Spend 15 min. today in a waiting - **silent** posture before the Lord – focus on the fullness of Joy.

2. Journal your thoughts.

<u>Day 4</u>

Accepting the Impossible assignments of God requires an assurance of His love, a clear "hearing" of His voice, and a faith to step out of your comfort zone into the impossible. Are you ready to move into a life filled with joy unspeakable?

Matthew 19:26 – But Jesus looked at them and said, "With man this is impossible, but with God all things are possible."

Job 42:2 - "I know that you can do all things, and that no purpose of yours can be thwarted.

1. Spend time today with "listening ears" for the Holy Spirits direction as to the "impossible" assignments that He may desire to stir within you.

2. Journal your thoughts

3. Decide today to make one step forward regarding one of the above assignments.

Day 5

His favor and open doors are promised to those who walk in His presence. Trusting Him to open those doors is an overwhelming experience. Things that aren't possible will begin to materialize as you step out in faith.

Proverbs 8:35 - For whoever finds me finds life and obtains favor from the Lord,

Revelation 3:8 - "I know your works. Behold, I have set before you an open door, which no one is able to shut. I know that you have but little power, and yet you have kept my word and have not denied my name."

1. What assignments need some open doors?

2. Spend time today waiting in His presence as you allow the Holy Spirit to direct you to the door handles that are prepared for you.

3. Journal your thoughts and directions of faith that were revealed to you during your **silent** time.

<u>Day 6</u>

Re-read <u>*Mission Possible*</u>.

1. What "Impossible" revelations and directions did you receive this week?

You are righteous!

<u>No Worries – Just Sing</u>

Watching the multitude of different birds that converge on my yard for their daily dance and song, I can't help but smile. Their symphony of different sounds begins with the sun and erupts as they fly in, take their quick turn at the feeders and move over for the next species.

They have no concern that it won't be there or won't be enough. They trust their provider to meet their daily needs.

No worries…just singing.

As the current seed provider, a smile and joy swell in my soul, causing me to ponder this sight. I can't help but wonder how our heavenly Father, our provider, must smile when He sees our trust.

His heart must swell with love as the understanding of His love for us, provision and constant attention to every detail in our lives, begins to register in our hearts. What a joy and smile we must bring to Him.

I can only imagine how He must feel when He sees us enjoying and trusting in His provisions with joy in our hearts and a song on our lips. I can almost hear Him say, "No Worries….Just Sing".

Day 1

Spend some time contemplating what _No Worries – Just Sing_ means to you.

1. What does this mean to you?

2. How does it apply to your life?

Day 2

Luke 12:22-31 - And he said to his disciples, "Therefore I tell you, do not be anxious about your life, what you will eat, nor about your body, what you will put on. For life is more than food, and the body more than clothing. Consider the ravens: they neither sow nor reap, they have neither storehouse nor barn, and yet God feeds them. Of how much more value are you than the birds! And which of you by being anxious can add a single hour to his span of life? If then you are not able to do as small a thing as that, why are you anxious about the rest? Consider the lilies, how they grow: they neither toil nor spin, yet I tell you, even Solomon in all his glory was not arrayed like one of these. But if God so clothes the grass, which is alive in the field today, and tomorrow is thrown into the oven, how much more will he clothe you, O you of little faith! And do not seek what you are to eat and what you are to drink, nor be worried. For all the nations of the world seek after these things, and your Father knows that you need them. Instead, seek his kingdom, and these things will be added to you.

1. As you contemplate the above scripture what areas of your own daily survival mode are you not trusting the Father to provide?

2. What does it mean to you to "Seek his kingdom"?

3. Spend time today laying down your anxious thoughts and concerns while you wait and listen to the Holy Spirits voice. Journal your thoughts.

Day 3

All of creation worships! As humans the ability to sing, dance and celebrate are exhibited at an early age. However, due to the struggles of life we tend to put those things away – thinking they are immature. But even King David rejoiced in the streets with song and dance. We as children of the King have so much to rejoice in – finding your voice and exuberant desire to celebrate brings freedom.

Psalm 108:3-4 - I will give thanks to you, O Lord, among the peoples; I will sing praises to you among the nations. For your steadfast love is great above the heavens; your faithfulness reaches to the clouds.

Psalm 89:1 - I will sing of the steadfast love of the Lord, forever; with my mouth I will make known your faithfulness to all generations.

Colossians 3:16 - Let the word of Christ dwell in you richly, teaching and admonishing one another in all wisdom, singing psalms and hymns and spiritual songs, with thankfulness in your hearts to God.

1. As a child, what were your favorite expressions of celebration?

2. How do you express those feelings now?

3. Take time today to try a new or past expression as you worship the Lord. Try singing out loud, shouting, dancing, skipping or whatever is stirring in your heart.

Day 4

Spring erupts with the sound of praise from every creature. Just as the birds sing out with praise - a thankful heart within us restores new life. Rejoicing in the presence of the Lord can feel foreign if you have hidden that away for sometime. Let's celebrate in the steadfast faithfulness of our God.

Psalm 34:1 - I will bless the Lord at all times; his praise shall continually be in my mouth.

Psalm 118:24 - This is the day that the Lord has made; let us rejoice and be glad in it.

Isaiah 55:12 - "For you shall go out in joy and be led forth in peace; the mountains and the hills before you shall break forth into singing, and all the trees of the field shall clap their hands.

1. Contemplate Isaiah 55:12 and journal nature's expressions of rejoicing.

2. Take time again today to express new ways of rejoicing in the presence of the Lord.

101

Day 5

Freedom and celebration come from a thankful heart. Our lives are filled with blessings and reasons to lift our voices in praise.

Children are so free to sing and dance. They jump at the chance to bang things together to make noise yet we adults – again, have shut that out and become "mature". Let's not – Let's celebrate again today and this time with noise.

Psalm 150:1-6 - Praise the Lord! Praise God in his sanctuary; praise him in his mighty heavens! Praise him for his mighty deeds; praise him according to his excellent greatness! Praise him with trumpet sound; praise him with lute and harp! Praise him with tambourine and dance; praise him with strings and pipe! Praise him with sounding cymbals; praise him with loud clashing cymbals! Let everything that has breath praise the Lord! Praise the Lord!

Psalm 33:3 - Sing to him a new song; play skillfully on the strings, with loud shouts.

1. List at least five things you are thankful for today and the impact they have on your life.

2. Worship with a new found freedom today. Celebrate with some NOISE!

Day 6

Re-read *No Worries – Just Sing*.

Thankful attitudes and rejoicing spirits are contagious to those around us. Keeping our eyes on Jesus, His faithfulness, His blessings and favor in our lives brings freedom to our souls and also changes the atmosphere in which we walk. Our "no worries – just singing" attitude can rub off on others. Wow, what a concept – making an impact on others for Christ! Let's adjust our attitudes to match our little feathered friends.

Psalm 100:2 - Serve the Lord with gladness! Come into his presence with singing!

Psalm 40:3 - He put a new song in my mouth, a song of praise to our God. Many will see and fear, and put their trust in the Lord.

1. As you have rejoiced through this week what changes have you seen and felt?

2. How can you implement a discipline of thankfulness and rejoicing in your life daily?

You are a child of the KING!

Encouragement Brings New Life

Words of affirmation and encouragement are building blocks to every heart. The words we speak to those around us can cut down or build up. Those words once spoken can never be taken back. So our choice daily is - which do we want to speak, words that build or words that hurt?

We can daily make choices to walk, leaning on and listening to the voice of the Holy Spirit and become true encouragers or allow our own words to gush forth in a tidal wave of emotion that usually will bring forth destruction.

I desire my words to heal, lift, bring a smile and change a life. Listening and speaking His words will bring life because true encouragement is the heart of the Father. If we make a choice to walk as an encourager we can bring His heart to our world.

<u>Day 1</u>

Spend some time contemplating what *<u>Encouragement Brings New Life</u>* means to you.

1. What does this mean to you?

2. How does it apply to your life?

Spring's Assurance

Day 2

The desire to be an encourager comes directly from a heart that loves. Being "others focused" needs to be our priority.

I Corinthians 13: 4-7 - Love is patient and kind; love does not envy or boast; it is not arrogant or rude. It does not insist on its own way; it is not irritable or resentful; it does not rejoice at wrongdoing, but rejoices with the truth. Love bears all things, believes all things, hopes all things, endures all things.

I John 2:10 - Whoever loves his brother abides in the light, and in him there is no cause for stumbling.

1. Think of a time that you have received encouragement from a friend. How did that directly impact you and how did you feel?

2. Could you tell this person loved you? What impact would it have had if it had been done in a judgmental harsh fashion?

107

Day 3

We all have opportunities to be encouragers but making a choice to speak in love to build up rather then tear down often isn't thought about until the opportunity is past. Practice being an encourager and those opportunities will become natural.

Colossians 3:12 - Put on then, as God's chosen ones, holy and beloved, compassionate hearts, kindness, humility, meekness, and patience,

I Thessalonians 5:11 - Therefore encourage one another and build one another up, just as you are doing.

1. Do you lean toward speaking quickly and sometimes harshly or do you stop, think and in love encourage?

2. Just as in all areas of our lives – stopping before speaking is a discipline we need to work at implementing. Spend time today and listen to the Holy Spirits direction regarding someone who can use encouragement today. Step out and love them with words of encouragement. A phone call, a lunch date or even a note can bring life to those who are struggling.

Day 4

Our words or words from others can and do cause division in relationships. Simple words of encouragement can break down walls that have brought distance between us and those we once called friends. Choices we make can change and lift up the hurting.

Romans 15:1-7 - We who are strong have an obligation to bear with the failings of the weak, and not to please ourselves. Let each of us please his neighbor for his good, to build him up. For Christ did not please himself, but as it is written, "The reproaches of those who reproached you fell on me." For whatever was written in former days was written for our instruction, that through endurance and through the encouragement of the Scriptures we might have hope. May the God of endurance and encouragement grant you to live in such harmony with one another, in accord with Christ Jesus, that together you may with one voice glorify the God and Father of our Lord Jesus Christ. Therefore welcome one another as Christ has welcomed you, for the glory of God.

Romans 12:18 - If possible, so far as it depends on you, live peaceably with all.

1. Think of someone that you may have offended or someone that has offended you. Lay the offence at the feet of Jesus and spend time today asking His direction regarding speaking encouragement to that person. Hear it – and do it.

2. Step out and connect with someone today that needs encouragement.

Day 5

Words are best used when they lift, heal and change a life.

Philippians 2:1-4 - So if there is any encouragement in Christ, any comfort from love, any participation in the Spirit, any affection and sympathy, complete my joy by being of the same mind, having the same love, being in full accord and of one mind. Do nothing from selfish ambition or conceit, but in humility count others more significant than yourselves. Let each of you look not only to his own interests, but also to the interests of others.

Philippians 4:8 - Finally, brothers, whatever is true, whatever is honorable, whatever is just, whatever is pure, whatever is lovely, whatever is commendable, if there is any excellence, if there is anything worthy of praise, think about these things.

1. Contemplate the above two scriptures. How can you implement them into your life to lift, heal and change lives by the use of your words?

2. Take time today and list things to think on that are honorable, just, pure, lovely, commendable, excellence and worthy of praise.

Day 6

Re-read *Encouragement Brings New Life.*

Proverbs 18:21 – Death and life are in the power of the tongue, and those who love it will eat its fruits.

1. What choices have you made this week that can allow your words to heal, lift and change lives around you?

You are highly favored!

"With This Ring"

"With this ring...." Is a phrase every couple repeats as they make a marriage commitment to each other. The meaning of those three little words has impact and significance that we rarely consider.

An intended bride waits in breathless anticipation for her beloved to extend his intent to make her his bride when he presents that sparkling ring.

He has willingly chosen to lay down his own life and give all he has for this one. His eyes and face shine with great joy and anticipation of the presentation and acceptance of this shining circle given as a token of all the love that he has exploding from within. Placing it on her finger signals her acceptance and desire to commit her life completely to him. Her eyes overflow with love and trust. Her glowing smile and giddy joy show no doubt in his acceptance of who she is.

The understood meanings of commitment, trust, love, and honor are all part of the acceptance of this shining symbol. However, these meanings we tend to ignore in our society. They are present nonetheless. Those meanings are the bride's acceptance of a new name as well as the power and authority that her new name and position hold.

We see the rich and famous signing prenuptial agreements in order to keep their own "things" to themselves – just in case.

Our groom; Jesus pours out lavishly upon his bride and ALL that is His belongs to us.

We, as the bride of Christ have also received this presentation of our bridegroom's signet ring. Thus acknowledging his eternal commitment, his poured out love and unconditional acceptance for us, his bride. We also have been given a new name that includes his power and authority.

Our understanding and use of what that means is rather overwhelming; but if we can receive this revelation our lives will be transformed as we walk in that given favor, power and authority that the name of Jesus Christ bought for us.

Our new name has already been proclaimed in heaven and that ring gives us HIS name and with that comes His power and authority. Everything that belongs to him belongs to us.

Let's accept and place that ring with all its authority upon our finger and move into the places He has called us to tread.

Day 1

Spend some time contemplating what *"With This Ring"* means to you.

1. What does this mean to you?

2. How does it apply to your life?

Day 2

Song of Solomon 4:9 - You have captivated my heart, my sister, my bride; you have captivated my heart with one glance of your eyes, with one jewel of your necklace.

1. The love expressed from a groom to his bride is one of unconditional acceptance. Express your understanding of this regarding Christ's acceptance of you – His lover, His bride.

2. Do you find your heart being tugged to "Come" - to draw close, to sit in His presence, to listen to His voice more often?

3. How can you adjust your life to allow time to run into that secret place when that call comes?

Day 3

I Peter 2:9 - But you are a chosen race, a royal priesthood, a holy nation, a people for his own possession, that you may proclaim the excellencies of him who called you out of darkness into his marvelous light.

1. As a chosen one, a royal priesthood, a Bride of the King what power and authority do we have?

2. Meditate on what it means to carry His name as our name – and that ALL that belongs to Him belongs to us. Journal your thoughts.

Day 4

Revelation 19:7 - Let us rejoice and exult and give him the glory, for the marriage of the Lamb has come, and his Bride has made herself ready;

Psalm 45:6 - Your throne, O God, is forever and ever. The scepter of your kingdom is a scepter of uprightness;

1. What does it mean to you   - that the "Bride has made herself ready"?

2. During the last 3 months how is your life being re-directed to a place of accepting the assurance of who Christ has created you to be?

Day 5

John 14:10-14 - Do you not believe that I am in the Father and the Father is in me? The words that I say to you I do not speak on my own authority, but the Father who dwells in me does his works. Believe me that I am in the Father and the Father is in me, or else believe on account of the works themselves. Truly, truly, I say to you, whoever believes in me will also do the works that I do; and greater works than these will he do, because I am going to the Father. Whatever you ask in my name, this I will do, that the Father may be glorified in the Son. If you ask me anything in my name, I will do it.

1. The realization of the authority that we carry in the name of Jesus Christ is one that can transform our lives and the atmosphere we live in if we step into that authority. Where have you been called into a new assignment that requires this authority?

2. What steps can you make this week to move off the sidelines and into the places He has called you to tread?

3. Spend time today praying into that and listening to His directions. Journal your thoughts.

Day 6

Re-read _"With This Ring"._

1. Spend some time today journaling your thoughts comparing the commitment, trust, love, honor, power, authority and favor given to us as the bride of Christ to that of a bride and groom in our current society.

You are His Beloved!

Notes

<u>Notes</u>

Titles available by J.K. Sanchez

Majestic Reflection Devotional Study Series:

Winters Rest

Spring's Assurance

Summer's Delight

Fall's Yield

Stand alone or companion journals:

Winters Rest Journal

Spring's Assurance Journal

Summer's Delight Journal

Fall's Yield Journal

Majestic Reflection Journal

Reflections of His Glory Journal

Additional Titles

Reflections of His Glory

Contact me at: Judy@jksanchez.com

Jksanchez.com

Also find me on Amazon.com

About the Author

J. K. Sanchez has lived and raised her three children in the Pacific Northwest where she and her husband of 40 years live and enjoy its beauty. As a writer and photographer her love of nature has flourished and is portrayed both through visually descriptive prose as well as through the eye of the camera.

Having ministered in many areas of the body of Christ her love for people and passion for worship and the presence of the Lord continually draw her to see freedom proclaimed and released to others through the finished work on the cross of Jesus.

www.ingramcontent.com/pod-product-compliance
Lightning Source LLC
Chambersburg PA
CBHW060303050426
42448CB00009B/1739